SILENCE OF THE LAMBS : THE TRUE STORY OF GARY HEIDNIK

FRANK STONE

Gary Heidnik was a serial killer whose rampage lasted from 1986-87. He built and designed a torture chamber in the basement of his home in North Philadelphia where he lured both prostitutes and mentally challenged adults, holding them captive for sex.

Heidnik constructed this house of horrors over the course of several months. He dug up the basement, bought chains to hold down the women and bars for the windows.

Experts are split on the verdict of whether Gary was pure evil or simply insane. What is certain, was that his goal was to have his own harem. A place where he could have his own "farm" of women who would give birth to his children.

He realized that no woman would undergo this voluntarily so he decided to begin abducting them, one by one, in the winter of 1986...

BIRTH OF A MONSTER

Gary grew up in the Eastlake suburb of Cleveland, Ohio, born to Michael and Ellen Heidnik on November 22nd, 1943. His parents would divorce when he was three years old. Gary and his younger brother Terry would then live with their mother for four years but she could not handle both the two young boys in her struggle with alcoholism. At the age of seven, both he and his brother were sent to live with their father who now had a new wife and family of his own.

"We came from Ohio," Gary's niece, Shannon recalled. "We're Pennsylvania Dutch, Irish, and something else. German, I think. The whole family was screwed up and weird. My mom told me how their dad beat Gary real bad with a toy wooden airplane because he peed his pants. His dad was an alcoholic, and his mom took poison. They found her in the basement. She was tired of the abuse. They were really sick parents, and they gave their kids some serious problems. Gary and my dad left Ohio at some point, and I'm not exactly sure how we wound up in Pennsylvania."

Gary and his father were always at odds. As a young boy, would wet his bed and his father would humiliate him by hanging his urine stained sheets outside his bedroom window. Gary would remain a lifelong bed-wetter.

Gary was insufferably shy in school and refused to talk to his fellow classmates. On one occasion, a girl felt sorry for him as no one ever spoke to him. She asked if he finished his homework and Gary responded by berating her.

"You're not worthy enough to talk to me," he screamed.

He also had a lump shaped head, which both he and his brother stated came as the result of falling out of a tree.

Despite his anti-social behavior, Gary had exceptional intelligence. He did well on school tests and was reported to have a genius level IQ of between 130-150. His father wanted him to attend a military academy as Gary would obsess about Army and Marine life. He would eventually drop out of high school and join the U.S. Army after he turned seventeen.

Highly intelligent, Gary adapted well to Army training. He stayed in the service for a little over a year and was graded "excellent" by his drill sergeant during basic training. Gary wanted to serve in the military police but his application was rejected as the Army would send him to medical training instead.

He received his medic certifications in San Antonio before being transferred to Landstuhl, West Germany where he would work at the 46th Army Surgical Hospital.

In August of 1962, Gary would not come into work at the hospital. Instead, he would be a patient, complaining of a severe headache, nausea and vomiting. After a physical examination, the physician on duty noticed that Gary also displayed symptoms of mental illness.

"In the '60s," prosecutor Charlie Gallagher said. "He went in the Army and he wanted to get a certain kind of training (military police), but they ended up training him as a medic. Then they sent him to Germany, and I think he didn't like the assignment, didn't like being in Germany. So he started thinking, "How can I beat this?" He just stopped obeying orders. He finally got them to give him a medical discharge. Eventually, he wound up with 100 percent disability, because he was able to convince the doctors that he was crazy. He's been faking all his life."

One of Gary's closest friends, John Cassidy, corroborates this story.

"I met Gary in '74 or '75 in Philly," Cassidy said. "He claimed the Army gave him LSD while he was in Germany. Sometime over there, he had a nervous breakdown. A legitimate, real nervous breakdown. And then he said he got this brilliant idea. He said, when he came out of it, why the hell should I come out of it if I can get disability?"

Two months after his initial complaint, he was transferred to a military hospital in Philadelphia where he was diagnosed as a schizophrenic.

The Army then honorably discharged him from service.

BACK IN SOCIETY

Re-entering civilian life, Gary found work as a licensed practical nurse (LPN) at a Veterans Administration hospital in Coatesville, PA. He exhibited rude and bizarre behavior towards patients, all of whom had mental issues themselves. He was fired from the hospital and then spent the next twenty-five years in and out of psychiatric facilities. Gary would claim to have tried to commit suicide over thirteen times.

As his niece stated, Gary came from a family where mental illness was the norm. His mother committed in 1970 when Gary was twenty-six. A lifelong alcoholic and depressive, she drank mercuric chloride to end her life.

His brother Terry's mental health wasn't much better than

his own as he also spent time in psychiatric facilities and tried to kill himself on numerous occasions.

A year after his mother's death, Gary turned to religion.

A religion of his own making.

He opened a church called the United Church of the Ministers of God. He started with only five followers, most of whom were mentally retarded adults from a nearby board and care facility.

"There was a sign on his house," Gallagher said. "United Church of the Ministers of God. He had an ID card as Bishop Heidnik, in a Roman collar. With the checks he was getting from the Army and Social Security, he started investing the money in his church's name. The first thing he invested in was Playboy ... and later he lost a lot of money on Crazy Eddie. Eventually, he changed $1,500 in investment money into three-quarters of a million dollars."

"He held these church services on Sundays," Gary's neighbor, Doris Zibulka said. "A lot of people came, and they were usually mentally retarded."

By 1986, Gary had over one million dollars in his account and he used the church as a tax shelter. He would drove around town in a Rolls Royce and a Cadillac, procuring African-American prostitutes.

"He formed his own religion after he left the Army," Cassidy said. "I believe it was originally just a tax scam, but towards the end, he was believing that stuff. I asked him, 'Don't you think if there's a God, he'll be upset with what you're doing to religion?' He said no, God would be amused. God has a sense of humor.'"

"In the '70s, he had this girlfriend, she was black and retarded. He has an IQ of 148, but all his girlfriends were black and retarded. He said the blacks treated him better than the whites ever did. He also said he sexually preferred blacks, that they expected less. His girlfriend was Anjeanette — I think they eventually had a daughter. And Anjeanette's sister was severely retarded, and he took her out of the institution and brought her home, and they said he kidnapped her."

Anjeanette's sister was named Alberta. Gary had signed her out of her mental institution and brought him to his home where he sexually assaulted her. She would later be found and returned to the mental institution in a traumatized state. A medical exam would reveal that she had been raped, sodomized and that Gary had given her gonorrhea.

Gary would be arrested and charged with kidnapping, multiple counts of rape, false imprisonment, and involuntary deviant sexual intercourse as Alberta was disabled.

This verdict would be overturned on appeal as the defense argued that Alberta was not mentally fit to testify.

Gary would spend two years in prison. During his hearing, he refused to speak when asked by the judge. His defense attorney grew upset and asked Gary why he was refusing to talk. The future killer then wrote in a note that "Satan shoved a cookie down my throat so I can't talk."

He would spend the next three years in a mental institution until his release in 1983.

FILIPINO MAIL ORDER BRIDES

Wanting to start his own family, Gary would use a mail order bride service to find a wife. He would have a pen pal relationship with Betty Disto for over two years before she arrived in the USA from the Philippines in 1985. Disto soon realized, however, that Gary was not a stable or faithful man as she found him in bed with three other women.

"After he got out of jail, he got this mail-order bride from the Philippines named Betty," Cassidy recalled. "He thought he was getting hooked up with a nice subservient Oriental, but she wasn't. He brought her up to the Franklin Diner a couple of times with me. He started getting much more reclusive around that time, though."

Disto would stick up for herself but was fearful of Gary as he raped and assaulted her on a daily basis. He forced her to watch as he had sex with prostitutes.

Neighbors would complain that they would hear Gary and his wife fighting a lot. They noted that after his wife left there would be hookers coming in and out of the home.

"One night we were sitting on the front porch," neighbor Zibulka said. "And a girl comes flying out the door — she was thrown out — she was half naked. She's screaming and banging on the door. The cops came, he gave her back the clothes."

Finally, with the aid of other Filipinos in the community, Betty was able to divorce Gary after a year of torture and abuse. Disto would give birth to a son after she left Gary, naming the boy Jesse John Disto.

Betty would later sue Gary for child support payments.

Gary would go on to have another child with women who were both illiterate and mentally disabled. He would have a son named Gary Jr but the baby was placed in foster care after his birth. He would have a daughter, Maxine, with Anjeanette Davidson but again the child was placed into foster care.

THE ABDUCTIONS BEGIN

On November 25th, 1986, Gary would abduct Josefina "Nicole" Rivera who at the time was working as a prostitute.

"Gary had picked me up the day before Thanksgiving," Nicole said. "It was cool, it was a little drizzly. It was the end of November so it was cold. It was chilly. He was tall. You could tell he was tall, you could tell he was tall in the car. He had dark brown hair and brown eyes. He didn't seem to be anything out of the ordinary."

"He wanted to go back to his house. That's something I don't really do. So he was the first exception I made to go to somebody's house. So we get to the house, we go upstairs. He gives me the money. We have sex. And then we're done and I get up and start to put my clothes on. And he just comes up behind me and starts choking me."

"It's like a broken film projector," Nicole said. "It's like your life just revolves, like chit, chit, chit (imitating the sound of a film projector). When I came to, he had a handcuff on my arm, on my wrist. He kept saying 'shut up, keep still, I'm not going to hurt you, I'm not going to hurt you.' He took me downstairs to the basement. He had a little hole dug in the basement. The music was blaring throughout the house. And he took muscle clamps with screws and he put them around my ankles, attached to a chain. He put the screws on with Crazy Glue. I was like, this is unbelievable. Is this really happening?"

DEHUMANIZATION

Gary then threw Nicole into a hole he had dug in the basement floor. She could not fit inside and he kept trying to smash her in. He took a large wooden board and slammed it on top of her, cramming her into the hole as if she were a bug.

He then placed a pair of heavy sandbags over the board.

Nicole continued to scream.

"I can't breathe! I can't breathe!"

Gary would then remove the sandbags and the board before lifting his victim out of the hole by her hair.

"Shut up!" he screamed, beating her with a stick. "Shut up! I'm not going to tell you again."

Gary would leave Nicole there for hours on end.

"When he first finally did take me out and he talked, he said that 'the goal was to have a bunch of women and a bunch of kids.' Because he said that the city or the state would not let him raise his own kids. And this way he could have a whole bunch of girls and get them all pregnant."

"When he took me out (of the pit) I could pretty much walk around. So he leaves and goes out and I could hear the car leaving. I was looking around and trying to figure out, how to get out, how to get help, whatever. He had this board thing on the wall, where somebody had nailed it, I pulled it and it came open and I crawled out through that thing. It was just enough room for me to get outside the house."

"So I'm outside the house and I'm hollering. I'm screaming at the top of my lungs. I was hollering in Spanish. I was hollering in English. And then I felt someone pulling the chains from behind me. And I'm like 'Oh my God, he's back.' And he pulled me back through that hole by the chain."

"'I need to do this better" Gary said then tightened it and re-clamped the restraints around Nicole's ankle with Crazy Glue.

Gary would leave Nicole in the hole for another twenty hours.

When he returned, he would have another woman with him.

"This is Sandra," Gary said. "Y'all are going to be down here awhile together so why don't you try to get along."

Sandra was not a prostitute, she was a mentally disabled adult he had gone to the store to get some medication for her pre-menstrual cramping.

She didn't return home that night.

Gary specifically targeted women who were "mentally challenged". He would impregnate two of them and the state would intervene, sending both children to foster care.

"He wanted women that he felt he was socially superior to," forensic psychologist Paula Orange said. "His personality required that someone look up to him, someone not to question him, and he found the perfect foil in this woman who lacked the mental capacity to know otherwise."

SANDRA LINDSAY

Gary had his eye on Sandra Lindsay for several years. He

would buy her dinner at McDonald's and she would attend his church.

Now she was a prisoner in his dungeon alongside Josefina Nicole Rivera.

"He was saying that he had known Sandy for four years and that she told him that she would have his baby," Nicole said. "But that she kept backing out of it. He would come down at different times and give us water and crackers. If he thought we were being bad or if someone was coming over to the house, he would stick us both in the hole and cover it with the board."

Sandy's family would contact police but they did not look into it because of Sandy's age. The reason was that Sandy was a twenty-five-year-old adult.

But law enforcement did not consider the fact that she was a mentally challenged adult, a trusting woman who could be taken advantage of.

Her family would call Cyril "Tony" Brown, Sandra's friend who unbeknownst to them worked as Gary's accomplice. Tony gave them the short shrift on the phone, saying that he knew nothing about Sandra. The family would then confront him at a local McDonald's, Sandy's favorite spot, and coerced him to give up Gary's number.

They then call the number of "The Bishop".

Gary cut the call short, telling Sandra's sister that she wasn't there and he hung up. The family still wasn't satisfied and showed up at Gary's front door.

He didn't answer the doorbell but they showed one of his neighbors a picture of Sandy and received confirmation that she had been there.

Gary's mind began to race for a solution. He needed to cover himself and throw the police off the trail of Sandra should they get nosy. He decided he would mail her family a Christmas card to put the police and her family at ease.

"Gary came down with a box of Christmas cards," Nicole

said. "He made Sandy write in the cards. He made her write, 'Dear Mom, I am all right, don't worry, Love Sandy.' Then he put on gloves, gave her a $20 bill, and he had her put it in the card. He wouldn't touch it himself"

Gary then drove from Philadelphia to New York just so he could mail the card from a distant postal address.

The card was taken the police.

"It was out of character for her to send a card and not call," Tracey Lomax, Sandy's sister said. "So we went back to Detective Armstrong and we asked him to have a handwriting analyst look at it. But he was content that she was okay. That's when he basically ceased the investigation."

MORE WOMEN REQUIRED

A few days before Christmas, Gary had abducted another woman, Lisa Thomas.

"He took me to City Line Avenue to TGI Friday's," Lisa recalled. "He had a martini and I had a cheeseburger and french fries. Then he took me to Sears and Roebucks and he told me to spend up to $50 ... then he took me to his house on Marshall Street and gave me a beer. We was watching a movie, then we went upstairs, and then we had sex. Afterward, he got up and strangled me. I couldn't hardly breathe. And I told him that he could do whatever he want, and that's when he got the handcuffs and took me down to the basement."

Seeing the bound Sandra and Nicole, Lisa realized she had entered a house of horrors.

And that she was the next victim.

"He had the chains and clamps," Lisa recalled. "He put them on my ankle, and he had to count the links so, you know, the amount to open my legs wide to have sex."

The women were then subject to daily rapes. On Christmas

day, he would feed the women Chinese food, which would be their final indulgence. In the days that followed, he kept his captives alive with Pop-Tarts in the morning and a plate of rice and hot dogs for dinner.

A week after Gary captured Lisa, he abducted another woman, named Debbie.

Debbie was another prostitute that would not have anyone looking for her if she went missing. She had the life profile that Gary needed and he followed the same modus operandi, luring her into the home as if were just an ordinary john, then choking her into unconsciousness.

Gary led her down to the basement and placed her in shackles with the rest of the girls.

Debbie, however, wouldn't cooperate. She screamed and hollered all night long. Gary would come down in the middle of the night and beat her a couple of times. One of the sticks he used had nails on the end which would leave wounds in her buttocks.

Needing more women, or perhaps getting an adrenaline rush, Gary continued to troll for prostitutes. He would find Jackie Askins and bring her back to his house of horror.

"He told me he would give me money to go with him for a half-hour," Jackie said. "When we got to his house, we was playing this video game called Mr. Do. And like a half-hour or 45 minutes later, he grabbed me in a headlock with his arm around my neck choking me. ... He took me to the basement, and I met Josefina (Nicole), Lisa, Debbie, Sandy."

HEAD GAMES

"Gary had a pathological need to feel superior to women," Orange said. "So the women he targeted were people he felt were beneath him. He started with a mail-order bride from the Philippines, then prostitutes, then mentally disabled women. He had that need to feel superior to them, to control them. Frankly, he probably thought they would be easier to control and he found out otherwise."

Gary tried to employ psychological techniques he learned in the Army on the women. He would force his victims to victimize each other when a perceived that a transgression took place.

"Gary would make us beat each other if one of us was bad," Nicole said. "At different times, I beat all of the other girls. Gary was handling us like we were in the military. At this time, all of the girls were back-biting each other trying to get in charge, because he would treat whoever was in charge better than the other girls."

His friend John Cassidy would later state that Gary would ask him if he could help him put up a fence at his house.

"He had (Nicole) with him," Cassidy said. "Gary and I had to run an errand in my truck, and I said that I didn't have room for her. He said she'll stay here at the gas station. Meanwhile, there were two police cars sitting there. She was supposed to be a captive. Well, she didn't seem like a captive. I know later they were talking about Stockholm syndrome or something. But she didn't appear to be a captive to me at all."

When the beatings didn't work, Gary would torture the women himself. He would gag the offender's mouth and press the tip of a screwdriver into her ears. He would start with a small screwdriver then work his way up to a bigger one. The girls would try and scream but the sounds come out muffled.

Around February and nearly three months of captivity, Gary became upset with Sandy. She was not eating her food fast enough for his liking and he ordered Lisa to beat her down. Lisa complied but still, Sandy chewed her food too slow. His anger raging, Gary then punched the young woman and hung her on a loop.

Sandy remained suspended for three days. Starved and feverish, she suffocated as when she was being held up by her arms, her oxygen was cut off.

"Gary took her chain off," Nicole recalled. "And he carried her body upstairs. I could see that Gary was upset. We were all upset because we didn't know what he was going to do. I was afraid that he would panic and take it out on all of us. Later on, we could hear a sound like an electric saw. Then we started to smell a terrible odor for like three or four days."

Gary chopped up her body parts but didn't know where he could place her arms and legs. He then wrapped them up the foil, marking the body parts as "dog food."

Gary then cooked her upper torso in the oven and placed her head inside a pot of boiling water. Neighbors called the police, complaining of the foul odor of burning flesh coming from Gary's home.

"I'm cooking a roast," Gary told the cops with a sheepish grin. "I fell asleep and it burnt."

Satisfied with his answer, the cops would leave him be.

Hearing the cops leave, Debbie began to holler and scream.

METHODS OF TORTURE

Upset that Debbie continued to be a nuisance, Gary stormed down into the cellar and grabbed her by the hair. He took her upstairs and showed her what he had done to Sandy.

He then returned Debbie to the storage pit. The young woman just sat there, her face ashen.

"She told me that Gary had Sandy's head in a pot on the stove and he was cooking it," Nicole said. "He had Sandy's ribs and, like, a hip bone in other pots in the oven. She also said that he had Sandy's arms and legs in the freezer in the kitchen."

Gary had shown Debbie just what would happen if she continued to cross him.

One of the methods Gary used to torture the women was with an electric shock. On one occasion, he would force three of the women, all bound in chains, into a pit of water in his basement. Gary then ordered Nicole to lay an electric current from a stripped extension cord to the women's chains.

"Gary told me to hook the hose up to the sink so he could fill the hole with water," Nicole recalled. "While the water was filling the hole, Gary went over to the electrical extension and he started to touch their chains with the hot wire. The girls were screaming and hollering, begging him to stop. Gary said he would stop if everybody got quiet, but Debbie refused to get quiet. Gary gave me the wire and told me to hold it on Debbie's chain. Debbie was still hollering, and then he took the wire from me and held it on Debbie's chain for a few minutes. Then everything went quiet."

Gary would later state that he never intended to kill Debbie. He thought that by keeping the woman grounded while she was being electrocuted she would only experience the current, the jolt of pain. Despite his high IQ, he didn't realize that the body doesn't respond to massive voltages of electricity in the matter he believed.

Gray then ordered Nicole to write a confession letter which stated that both he and Nicole had electrocuted Debbie. He informed Nicole that now he could trust her because he had that letter.

He then took Nicole out with him, looking for a place to dump Debbie's body.

"We pulled into a little place," Nicole recalled. "Like a little driveway, and Gary said, 'This is it This is where I am going to place Deborah's body at.' He walked a good ways into the park because he didn't want anybody to find it that was just like strolling through the park or something."

REPLACEMENT NEEDED
Nicole's survival instincts had kicked in and she learned how to acquiesce to Gary's demands without punishment. He began

to trust her and he allowed Nicole to accompany him as he went to abduct more women. She was his accomplice on March 23rd, 1987 as he kidnapped Agnes Adams. Nicole would later use this as an opportunity to get help.

"Gary put the girls down in the hole and we went out looking for girls," Nicole said. "While we were on Girard, we passed by a girl I know, Agnes. Gary told me that if I helped him pick her up after he finished with her, he would let me contact my family. After they finished having sex, he took her down to the basement. And then he asks me if there is another girl I could get. I told him I had proved myself to him and that I had to get the girl by myself. I told him to wait at the gas station at 6th and Girard, that this girl lived a couple of blocks away and I had to walk up to her house myself. He agreed to this, and I left him in the car at 6th and Girard. I walked away and I ran to my house, and my boyfriend opened the door and asked where I had been. I tried to tell him what had happened and he told me I was crazy. Then I went to the phone booth on the corner."

But her story was so bizarre that the police did not believe it at first. They interrogated her repeatedly and she did not vary any details. They arrived on the scene, examined the bruises and chafing on her leg, then became convinced she was telling the truth.

The police converged on Gary at the gas station and arrested him.

"She said he's up the corner, at 6th and Girard," Police officer John Cannon recalled. "I said, well, let's see if Mr. Gary's up there … and sure enough, there was a Cadillac, just like she described. We got out, approached, ordered him out of his car. The girl came down and said,
'Yeah, that's him, that's him. He raped me and killed these two other girls, and he had me eating her bones. He cut up this girl and put her in a pot and made us eat her.' She said other girls were still in there, down in the cellar in a hole. I said, 'Wow.'"

Nicole would then lead the police to Gary's residence. The home had metal doors on it and the windows had bars, giving it the look of an urban prison.

Officers approached and heard the television blasting at full volume. Breaking in, they were led down to the cellar door.

Inside, they saw half-naked women chained the floor.

"We're saved," the women screamed. "We're saved."

"I went right to the freezer in the kitchen," police lieutenant James Hansen said. "Josefina (Nicole) had said he had body parts in there. So I open the freezer, and I went to enough autopsies to know they were body parts. Then I proceed down to the basement, and the girls are sitting on a mattress, they were in shock, naked. They were chained to a soil pipe, padlocked. We had to go to the firehouse and get bolt cutters."

TRIAL AND SENTENCING

Police would later arrest Gary's accomplice, Cyril "Tony" Brown but would release him on the agreement that he would testify against Gary.

Gary would try to hang himself in jail but was unsuccessful. He would be brought to trial and his attorney would use legal insanity as a defense. This was rebuffed by the prosecution who argued that Gary had over $550,000 (one million dollars adjusted for inflation) in his bank and brokerage accounts. His financial advisor would be called in to testify and would state that Gary was "an astute investor who knew exactly what he was doing."

Gary would be sentenced to death and was jailed at the State Correctional Institution in Pittsburgh. He would attempt suicide twice, once by hanging and another by an overdose of his prescribed Thorazine.

Strangely, his daughter Maxine and ex-wife Betty would file suit and seek a stay of his execution, stating that he was mentally competent. Gary would overrule his family, however.

Gary didn't want to appeal the death sentence.

"He was smart enough to know he was not getting acquitted," Gary's defense lawyer Chuck Peruto said. "He had a motive not to fight the death sentence. Look at the type of crime he committed, and all of his victims were black. He was getting his ass kicked every single fucking day in jail. So it was either a lifetime of getting your ass kicked — and I'm not talking about punched — or the death penalty."

Gary would be executed by lethal injection on July 6th, 1999.

bonus story:

    Christa Gail Pike, born 10 March 1976, currently sits on Tennessee's death row for the murder of Colleen Slemmer, 19, on 12 January 1995. The murder occurred when Pike was 18 years old. Pike and her then-boyfriend Tadaryl Shipp who was 17 at the time of the murder were convicted of Slemmer's murder and conspiracy to commit murder. Another friend of the defendants and the victim, Shadolla Peterson, also 18 at the time, was convicted as an accessory after the fact and given six years' probation after turning informant. Pike was sentenced to death by electrocution in 1996 and, at the time, she had the distinction of being the youngest woman ever to be sentenced to death, in any state and only the second women given the death penalty in Tennessee.

Early Life

Pike's life reads like a primer for depraved murderers. As a small child, Pike did not enjoy a healthy and supportive bond with her mother, Carissa Hansen, a licensed nurse, allegedly because of her premature birth. Whereas thousands of children are born prematurely and do not resort to criminal behavior Pike's birth was presented as evidence of one possible origin of her poor and troubled behavior. Pike's maternal grandmother was verbally abusive and Pike was raised by her alcoholic and abusive paternal grandmother until the latter's death in 1988 when Pike was

12; after which Pike attempted suicide by overdosing. She was then shuttled back and forth between her divorced parents' homes. In 1989, Pike was kicked out of her father's house for the second and final time due to her unruliness and the alleged sexual abuse of her father's then-two-year old daughter with his second wife.

Prior to the murder, experts assert that there were myriad indications that Pike was seriously disturbed; however, nobody who may have suspected this sought help for the increasingly disobedient and incorrigible young lady. According to Pike's mother, she was problematic since the age of eight and the two of them had a contentious relationship due to Pike's fluctuating and troubling behavior. Her mother asserted that by age nine Pike was growing marijuana in pots at their home and had been permitted to have a live-in boyfriend at age 14. At one point—in an effort to improve their relationship—Hansen suggested that she and Pike smoke marijuana together. Hansen mistakenly believed that cultivating a friendship with her daughter would cultivate the necessary bond Pike had been lacking her entire life. At one point, one of her mother's boyfriends whipped Pike with a belt which prompted her to wield a butcher knife against him before he was subsequently arrested. Hansen also admitted that Pike had repeatedly lied to and stolen from her. In several interviews with Hansen throughout Pike's trial and seemingly endless appeals, she admitted repeatedly that she was a terrible mother and should have spent more time with her daughter.

Pike's aunt, Carrie Ross, provided insight into Pike's upbringing when she testified that she disallowed her own children from associating with Pike because she lived in a filthy house that had zero ground rules and that Pike was a pathological liar of whom she was somewhat afraid. She also admitted that there was a history of substance abuse in Pike's family. Ross also stated that on the few occasions that Pike actually visited her she behaved like a little girl and engaged in Barbie and dress-up play with her eleven-year-old cousin. Further, there were some allegations that Pike may have been sexually abused but these were neither confirmed nor denied.

Pike's father, Glenn Pike testified that he did, in fact, kick his daughter out of his house multiple times; the last time being in 1989 after the aforementioned allegations that Pike sexually abused her two-year old half-sister. He admitted that he had signed adoption papers for Pike prior to her 18th birthday and that during the times she resided with him she was manipulative, disobedient, and dishonest.

After dropping out of high school, Pike began Job Corps classes in computer programming. Job Corps is a government-based organization that provides occupational and vocational training to underprivileged and troubled teens. It was at the now-defunct Job Corps center in Knoxville where she met Shipp, Slemmer, and Peterson. While Job Corps seeks to promote prosocial behavior and foster a strong desire among its participants to learn a vocation and secure a more promising future than might have been previously the case, this program is also known to cultivate criminal activity, likely due to the association among its participants; many of whom already had problematic behavior.

Evidence of Premeditation

On 11 January 1995, the day before the actual homicide, Pike told friend and co-Job Corps student Kim Iloilo that she was planning to kill Slemmer because she "just felt mean that day." Iloilo discounted Pike's statement as nothing more than merely talk; however, the following evening at approximately 8:00 p.m. Iloilo witnessed Pike, Shipp, Peterson, and Slemmer leaving the Job Corps center. When Iloilo saw Pike, Shipp, and Peterson returning at approximately

10:15 p.m. without Slemmer she, again, thought nothing of it. Even when Pike visited Iloilo's dorm room at 11:00 p.m. that night and confessed to killing Slemmer—as well as showing Iloilo what Pike identified as a piece of Slemmer's skull—Iloilo still failed to tell anyone. Later, at Pike's trial, Iloilo testified that while Pike was iterating the events of the murder she was oddly smiling, singing, and dancing around the room. The following morning Iloilo asked Pike what she was going to do with the piece of skull. Pike nonchalantly replied that she had it in her pocket and was, in fact, eating breakfast with it.

Pike also told another student, Stephanie Wilson, a similar account the following day and proudly described the brown spots on her shoes as blood. Not unlike Iloilo, Wilson failed to immediately report anything.

The Crime Scene

On 13 January, officers from the University of Tennessee and Knoxville Police Departments were dispatched to greenhouses on the University's agricultural campus in Tyson Park where a University grounds department employee reported finding, at approximately 8:05 a.m., what he assumed to be a dead animal. The gruesome discovery was a corpse that turned out to be Colleen Slemmer. She was naked from the waist up; her throat was cut; her head had been bludgeoned; and she had various cuts all over her arms, throat, and torso—including a pentagram that had been carved into her chest. Officer John Terry Johnson who testified at Pike's trial described Slemmer's body as so badly beaten that she was unrecognizable as a human being. He also stated that he thought he was looking at her face when, in reality, Slemmer was lying face-down in the dirt and debris where Pike, Shipp, and Peterson had left her.

There was additional evidence and testimony that the crime scene encompassed an area that measured 100 feet long by 60 feet wide; an astounding 6,000 square feet in area. Despite the area being muddy and wet there was ample evidence of a physical struggle with trampled bushes, a considerable amount of blood, body drag marks, and hand and knee prints. Thirty feet from Slemmer's body was a large pool of blood which suggested that Slemmer was attacked in one area and then dragged to where her body was later found. Slemmer's shirt and bra were also discovered at the crime scene, as well as a bloody rag that Pike admitted to tying over Slemmer's mouth at one point to keep her from screaming.

Disturbingly, University of

Tennessee police officer Harold James Underwood, Jr., who was the officer assigned to secure the crime scene, testified at trial that Pike and a few other females came to the scene between four and five p.m. the day of the discovery and before Pike was even considered to be a suspect. Underwood stated that Pike had asked why the wooded area was marked off, who the victim was, and whether police had any leads as to who the suspect or suspects were. He particularly recalled Pike's odd behavior—moving around a lot while giggling amusedly—and that she wore a necklace in the shape of a pentagram. The following day, during briefing when informed

that the victim had a pentagram carved
into her chest, Underwood reported
Pike's behavior and necklace to his
supervisors.

Autopsy and Findings

During Slemmer's autopsy, the
medical examiner, Dr. Sandra Elkins,
had to identify the victim's body from
dental records because her head was so
bludgeoned that she was
unrecognizable. After cleaning up
Slemmer's body which was clad only in
jeans, socks, and shoes, and covered
with dirt and twigs, Dr. Elkins began
cataloging Slemmer's wounds. Due to
the sheer number of wounds on her
back, arms, abdomen, and chest, and
the fact that following department

policy which stated that each individual wound be assigned a letter of the alphabet, when Dr. Elkins reached double letters she, instead, individually catalogued only the most serious wounds and that there were innumerable other superficial and defensive wounds. Among the most serious cuts was a six-inch gaping wound across Slemmer's throat that was deep enough to penetrate the fat and muscles in her neck as well as the aforementioned pentagram. Additional injuries included fresh bruising which Dr. Elkins asserted was consistent with crawling.

Cause of death was ultimately attributed to blunt force trauma to the head. Dr. Elkins surmised that Slemmer's head was hit with the asphalt at least four times—two to the left side, one over the right eye, and one to the nose—which collectively resulted in multiple and extensive skull fractures. One of these blows was to the left side of Slemmer's head—which, according to Dr. Elkins, occurred with the right side of the victim's head against a firm surface. This blow only fractured her skull but also imbedded a portion of Slemmer's skull into her head and contained black particles from the piece of asphalt determined to be the murder weapon.

Even more tragic was Dr. Elkins'

findings that none of Slemmer's other wounds would have rendered her unconscious and evidence of active blood flow around the wounds and blood in her sinus cavity indicated that Slemmer was alive during the severe torture she suffered before being killed.

Arrest and Confession

The police quickly connected Pike to the homicide thanks to the piece of Slemmer's skull discovered in Pike's jacket pocket. Pike had left this jacket hanging on the back of a chair in Job Corps Orientation Specialist Robert A. Pollock's office on 13 January after meeting with him about a misplaced ID card. Pike's jacket remained in Pollock's office from 4:00 p.m. on 13 January until 7:30 a.m. on 17 January. After learning over the weekend that Pike was a suspect in Slemmer's murder investigation, Pollock immediately gave the jacket to William Hudson, the Job Corps' safety and security captain who turned it over to Knoxville Police Department Officer Arthur Bohanan. At trial, Bohanan would testify that he found a small piece of bone in one of the pockets and presented it to Dr. Murray Marks, a University of Tennessee forensic anthropologist who was reconstructing Slemmer's decapitated skull and the piece in Pike's jacket pocket fit perfectly into an area where a portion of her skull was missing at the time of the victim's discovery.

When confronted with this evidence and subsequently arrested, Pike waived her *Miranda* protections and confessed to the murder and permitted officers to search her dorm room where the blood-soaked jeans she wore the previous night were found. Additionally, Pike led officers to a trash can at a nearby Texaco station on Cumberland Avenue where she had disposed of Slemmer's ID and a pair of gloves Pike had been wearing at the time of the homicide.

Pike's transcribed confession was 46 pages long.

In it, Pike admitted that there was animosity between Slemmer and her because Pike was convinced that Slemmer was a rival for the affections of her boyfriend, Shipp, and that Slemmer was trying to get Pike kicked out of the Job Corps program so she could have Shipp for herself. Pike also claimed that she had awakened one night to find Slemmer standing above her with a box cutter; however, there is no evidence of this allegation. Instead, Slemmer had repeatedly called her mother, May Martinez, to tell her she was afraid of Pike who she had awakened to find in her room and that she wanted to come home; to which Slemmer's mother said that she couldn't because she had signed a contract. Pike stated that she had only planned to fight Slemmer to stop her from running her mouth. On that fateful night of 12 January, Pike, Slemmer, Shipp, and Peterson signed the Job Corps logbook as they were leaving for an outing Slemmer believed was to smoke marijuana en route to a video store so that Pike and she could try to work out their problems.

When the group entered a tunnel at the edge of Tyson Park, Slemmer likely felt that something was not quite right and proceeded to ask Pike where they were going and whether there was, in fact, any marijuana. These questions irritated Pike who began the

brutal assault shortly thereafter
after they had gone deeply enough into
the woods so that nobody could hear
them that led to Slemmer's murder.

Pike confessed to initially
slamming Slemmer's head into her knee
and then throwing her to the ground
where Pike continually punched,
kicked, and slammed Slemmer's head
into the concrete, screaming, "the
bi*ch won't die" and that she wanted
"to see [Slemmer's] brains flow."
According to witnesses Shipp and
Peterson, as Slemmer continued to
plead with Pike to stop, Pike got
angrier and more brutal. Slemmer
offered to return to her Florida home,
leave her belongings at the Job Corps

center, and not tell anyone what happened; however, Pike became more enraged and yelled at Slemmer to be quiet because "it was harder to hurt someone who was talking to you."

In addition to the savage beating, Slemmer had been cut innumerable times with a box cutter and a mini meat cleaver (that Pike had allegedly borrowed from another Job Corps student) to her torso, arms, face, and back including having had her throat slit six times prior to the fatal blow that resulted from having her head crushed by a piece of asphalt. There was also a pentagram carved into Slemmer's chest; however, Pike asserted that Shipp had done that.

Pike also confessed to "just watching Slemmer bleed" when the victim got up and tried to run away. Pike admitted to cutting Slemmer's back: "the big long cut."

After the murder, Pike stated that she and Shipp washed their hands and shoes in a nearby mud puddle to conceal the blood, dumped the box cutter, and Pike returned the meat cleaver to the person from which she borrowed it. This person has never been identified.

The physical evidence and co-defendant testimony suggested that the assault and murder lasted from 30 minutes to an hour and consisted of Slemmer repeatedly trying to get up and run away but was prevented from doing so by the co-defendants who also, as Pike testified, contributed to the physical assault by throwing rocks at Slemmer's head and holding her down so she couldn't run away. Later, Pike would testify that she heard voices in her head overriding Slemmer's continual screaming, telling her that she needed to prevent Slemmer from filing charges against her for attempted murder. Pike also admitted that at one point she thought she had heard a noise and went to investigate it to ensure that they were alone, as well as alleging that during the assault she heard Slemmer breathing in blood and jerking but did not let this assuage her anger as Pike continued her savagery.

Even more troublesome, a police video recorded after Pike's confession shows Pike smiling and providing extensive details about the crime at the crime scene, oftentimes mimicking her actions that evening. Many have said that her demeanor on the recording was eerily similar to that of a little girl who was excited and happy that she had experienced the best day of her life and had no problem talking about the events that transpired, the heinousness of her actions, and how she felt about it all.

The facts of the homicide are not

nor have they ever been in dispute, thanks to an abundance of evidence. Pike's confession, and witness testimony at the trial.

Pre-Trial Examination

Prior to her trial, Pike was given a battery of assessment tests and examined by numerous psychiatrists including clinical psychologist Dr. Eric Engum who found her to be extremely bright as evidenced by an I.Q. of 111—in the 77th percentile of the general population—which he believed to be remarkable given her difficult childhood and lack of formal schooling beyond the ninth grade. Dr. Engum also found that Pike had excellent reasoning, problem solving, language, and analytic skills, and was also quite adept at paying attention, sustaining concentration, and sequencing information. Dr. Engum concluded that Pike was legally sane and had no brain damage which has frequently been demonstrated to cause violent behavior in some individuals.

Of particular interest was that Pike was found to be marijuana- and inhalant-dependent and also diagnosed with borderline personality disorder. Whereas there are some similarities between borderline personality disorder and antisocial personality disorder such as impulsivity, irritability, aggression, and a self-image that fluctuates between self-aggrandizement and despair, there are several differences. Individuals with borderline personality disorder differ from those with antisocial behavior in that the former—which primarily affects females—is characterized by a lack of remorse, self-destructiveness, black-and-white thinking, alcohol and/or drug use or abuse, unstable relationships characterized by fear of abandonment and extreme swings between love and hate, difficulty in achieving academic and vocational goals, and are more likely to have been sexually abused; while the latter—which affects disproportionately more males—is characterized by a lack of affect and remorse, emptiness, and an ultimate goal of self-preservation.

Pike demonstrated all of the aforementioned characteristics of borderline personality disorder which makes it easier—but not justifiably so—to comprehend how her intense jealousy of Slemmer and fear of losing Shipp made her commit her atrocious acts. In addition to her fear of abandonment, Pike also abused drugs, was likely sexually abused, had contentious relationships, and displayed zero remorse. Dr. Engum surmised that Pike did not act with premeditation or deliberation in Slemmer's murder but, instead, in a manner that was consistent with borderline personality disorder. More simply, Pike had lost control. However, on cross-examination Dr. Engum admitted that Pike's deliberate luring of Slemmer, that she carved a pentagram in the victim's chest, that she brought weapons with her, and that she bashed Slemmer's head into the concrete does, in fact, constitute deliberateness.

That Pike was overjoyed and singing in Iloilo's room describing the murder while dancing around with the portion of Slemmer's skull Pike had taken as a trophy further supported Dr. Engum's diagnosis of borderline personality disorder because she had eliminated who she perceived was in competition for her boyfriend, Shipp, and, therefore, could continue her relationship with him. When questioned about the piece of skull Pike had taken, Dr. Engum said that Pike had no identity and her actions of taking and displaying the skull was a way to get recognition, no matter how misleading and distorted said recognition might be. In fact, after her conviction and sentencing Pike wrote a letter to Shipp which was intercepted by jail personnel that stated that even though she tried to be "nice" to Slemmer by bashing in her head instead of letting her bleed to death she was still sentenced to "fry."

The Trial

There was an abundance of evidence

presented at the trial. Physical evidence consisted of crime scene photographs, autopsy reports, bloody clothing, and the piece of Slemmer's skull Pike had taken as a trophy. With respect to this skull piece, Dr. Elkins presented Slemmer's decapitated skull that was reconstructed by Dr. Marks to explain the victim's injuries. The skull presented at trial was complete except for a portion that was missing on the left side of Slemmer's skull. Dr. Elkins demonstrated that the piece of skull found in Pike's jacket fit perfectly into this spot, much to the chagrin of Slemmer's mother who, in a taped interview, stated that Pike was oftentimes giggling and passing notes to her mother and defense attorney during the trial, not unlike an immature middle-schooler.

At the trial, the State introduced photographs taken of Pike and Shipp at the Knoxville Police Department in which both were wearing pentagram necklaces similar to the shape carved into Slemmer's chest. It was presented that both Pike and Shipp dabbled in devil worshiping and other forms of the occult and that Slemmer was a sacrifice for the next day, Friday the 13th. Despite the presence of some type of satanic elements in Slemmer's murder, Dr. William Bernet, Vanderbilt University's psychiatric hospital medical director, testified that the evidence was that of "an adolescent dabbling in Satanism." He further concluded that the concept of collective aggression—or mob mentality—in which a group of people become stimulated and subsequently engage in some type of violent behavior was most assuredly at play in the events leading to Slemmer's death. However, Dr. Bernet ultimately stated that he did not have enough evidence to definitively surmise whether Pike had acted with premeditation or intent when she lured and murdered Slemmer.

Pike was ultimately convicted of first-degree murder and conspiracy to commit first-degree murder after a mere two-and-a-half hours of jury deliberation. The fact that the jury returned guilty verdicts for first-degree murder—and did it so quickly—demonstrate that jurors were convinced that Pike had the requisite mens rea, or mental capacity, to warrant a first-degree murder charge: premeditation and deliberation. Amidst the overwhelming evidence and utter lack of remorse for her actions Pike was sentenced to death by electrocution (Tennessee has since adopted lethal injection for executions but has the prerogative to utilize electrocution if the lethal injection drugs cannot be obtained). Shipp was sentenced to life without parole because his age at the time of the murder was too young to warrant capital punishment and Peterson turned informant and was given six years' probation for her testimony.

Pike's conviction was upheld by the Court of Criminal Appeals and the United States Supreme Court denied certiorari.

Post-Conviction

While incarcerated, Pike demonstrated more evidence of her depravity. In 2001 she tried to murder fellow inmate Patricia Jones by strangling her with a shoelace. Pike alleges that Jones repeatedly tortured her by calling her "fried chicken" and making various demeaning sounds as an affront to what Jones said was the sound that Pike would make when she was electrocuted. The final straw was when Jones physically threatened Pike's friend, fellow devil worshiper Natasha Cornet. Pike said that she jumped atop Jones and choked her with a shoelace so that the much larger and heavier Jones would get off of Cornet. By the time prison guards reached them, Jones was unconscious.

Pike was subsequently convicted of attempted murder despite her prior death sentence because any offense committed while an individual is incarcerated must be adjudicated. During this time, neurology specialist Dr. Jonathan Henry Pincus began investigating Pike's brain to glean some type of knowledge as to why Pike behaved and continued to act violently the way she did when she assaulted Jones. He asserted that every killer he has ever examined share three commonalities: brain damage, a history of abuse, and mental illness. Dr. Pincus alleged that Pike did, in fact, possess all three features and demonstrates all of the requisite features common to serial killers. There is much consensus among professionals that Pike would likely have been a serial killer had she not been caught the first time.

He also testified at Pike's attempted murder trial that her

brain's frontal lobes are not "put together properly"; largely due, he claimed, to the fact that Pike's mother drank while she was pregnant with Pike despite denial of this by Pike's mother. It was also brought up that as a child Pike played at the slaughterhouse where her grandfather worked and that she was frequently subjected to pornography and horror movies on the home television screen. He asserted that all of these factors provide insight into how an 18-year old girl could act with such depravity as was the case when Pike murdered Slemmer. However, the original trial judge, Mary Beth Leibowitz, stated that Pincus' "findings" of brain damage was curious as the defense expert at Pike's original trial who was trying to spare her the death penalty failed to find such evidence.

Forensic psychiatrist William Kenner testified that Pike had suffered from undiagnosed bipolar disorder, the symptoms of which were evident from the time Pike was a "sleepless, talkative adolescent" and likened her to an automobile with cruise control set at 120 miles per hour. Pike's post-conviction defense team alleged that this non-diagnosis justified her requesting a new trial.

In 2002 Pike sought to have her appeal legally stopped and to proceed with her execution. In June of that year Judge Leibowitz granted Pike's request and scheduled an execution date of 19 August 2002. However, a few days later Pike changed her mind and the Tennessee Court of Appeals subsequently stayed her execution. In October 2005, Pike's death sentence was affirmed; however, no execution date has been set at this time.

Pike was again in court in 2007 when her defense team headed by Donald E. Dawson asserted sought a new trial, alleging ineffective assistance of counsel in that her trial defense team failed to introduce evidence supporting Pike's alleged bipolar disorder. During this hearing, Shipp admitted to misinforming investigators and that he, in fact, was primarily responsible for Slemmer's murder. He stated that he was drunk and tired and just wanted the police to leave him alone when he put the onus of blame on Pike. Additional testimony from prior Job Corps student and the defendants' mutual friend Tyrone Comfort stated that Shipp controlled and abused Pike despite her assertions that he was the first male to protect her and she admired the respect and fear he elicited from others. Pike, however, was heavily medicated during this hearing for her alleged bipolar condition and the hearing was rescheduled for April 2008.

During her 2008 hearing,

prosecutors portrayed Pike as a cold-blooded vicious killer who not only planned Slemmer's murder but prolonged it for sport, essentially playing cat-and-mouse with Slemmer by allowing her to get up and try to escape and then pushing her back on the ground for additional torture. Ultimately, her request for a new trial was denied.

Pike became newsworthy again in 2012 when she formulated an escape plan with the help of 34-year-old New Jersey resident Donald Kohut who frequently visited Pike in prison but the extent of their relationship remains unknown, and 23-year-old former prison guard Justin Heflin. In a joint investigation by the Tennessee

Department of Corrections, the Tennessee Bureau of Investigation, and the New Jersey State Police after receiving information about the plan, both men were arrested and charged with bribery and conspiracy to commit escape, with Heflin charged with an additional facilitation to commit escape charge due to his job as a prison guard. Authorities discovered contraband evidence in the facility which could have only been brought in by a staff member and that Heflin was likely involved. Further investigation demonstrated that Heflin knew Kohut and that Heflin was receiving gifts and money for his assistance in the escape plan. Pike was also charged.

Even more recently, during yet another post-conviction relief hearing in 2015, testimony revealed that Pike was allegedly pregnant at the time of the murder. While this may be true it neither excuses her actions nor provides any potential evidence of legal insanity to justify an affirmative defense of not guilty by reason of mental disease or defect or guilty but mentally ill. Also during this hearing, Slemmer's mother requested the missing piece of her daughter's skull so she could bury the whole of her daughter but was denied as the skull piece remains a critical piece of evidence in Pike's ongoing legal appeals.

Since exhausting the state appeal process, Pike's new defense attorney, Assistant Federal Defender Stephen A. Ferrell, filed a 123-page petition on her behalf alleging that he constitutional rights were violated in both the original 1996 trial and penalty phase and that Tennessee's appellate courts ignored said violations. Among these claims is that capital punishment would amount to cruel and unusual punishment in violation of the Eighth Amendment of the United States Constitution because of Pike's youth, immaturity and mental illness. While Shipp—only 17 at the time of the murder—was too young to warrant imposition of a death sentence, Pike was not. Ferrell alleged that her trial lawyers were incompetent and failed to introduce evidence of mental illness, brain injury, and post-traumatic stress disorder. In response, the state Attorney General submitted a 90-page rebuttal repeatedly asserting that the state courts' ruling were all legally correct. As of the beginning of 2016, this battle continues.

Numerous video interviews of Pike over the past several years show her admitting that she was fully cognizant of her actions and that they were wrong. She stated that she felt as though she was taking out years of abuse on Slemmer and that she committed a horrible atrocity and deserves to be punished; however, she asserts that she deserves life without the possibility of parole for her actions; not the death penalty for the actions of three individuals. She has repeatedly stated that she wishes it was she who died and not Slemmer but such protestations are moot after the fact. One cannot help but wonder if Pike actually means what she says or is simply saying what she thinks others want to her. Knoxville Police Department detective Randy York who worked the case has said that in his lengthy career he has not encountered many people who he believes are evil but that Pike is, indeed, the personification of evil and that she should never be permitted to be around other human beings ever again.

Experts assert that the death penalty is not an effective general deterrent and debate over the morality and legality of capital punishment remains contentious and in the forefront of public discourse and debate. Currently, Tennessee is only one of 38 states which have the death penalty. Whereas women comprise 13% of those arrested for murder, only 2% are sentenced to death and, of those, only 3% are actually executed; primarily due to judges not wanting to sentence women to death. In Tennessee, only two individuals on death row have been executed—both males. The last time a woman was executed in the state was in 1837. Many currently believe that Pike will likely never be executed.

35869607R00041

Made in the USA
Middletown, DE
17 October 2016